STEM *trailblazer* BIOS

FLICKR COFOUNDER AND WEB COMMUNITY CREATOR CATERINA FAKE

PATRICIA WOOSTER

Lerner Publications Company
Minneapolis

Lerner Publications Company
A division of Lerner Publishing Group, Inc.
241 First Avenue North
Minneapolis, MN 55401 USA

For reading levels and more information, look up this title at www.lernerbooks.com.

Content Consultant: Karen North, Ph.D., Director, Annenberg Program on Online Communities, University of Southern California

Library of Congress Cataloging-in-Publication Data

Wooster, Patricia.
    Flickr cofounder and web community creator Caterina Fake / Patricia Wooster.
        p.   cm — (STEM trailblazer bios)
    Includes index.
    ISBN 978-1-4677-2460-9 (lib. bdg. : alk. paper)
    ISBN 978-1-4677-2490-6 (eBook)
    1. Fake, Caterina, 1969– —Juvenile literature. 2. Web site development—Juvenile literature. 3. Computer programmers United States—Biography—Juvenile literature. 4. Flickr (Electronic resource)—Juvenile literature. I. Title.
    TK5102.56.F34W66 2014
    005.1092—dc23 [B]   2013028641

Manufactured in the United States of America
1 – PC – 12/31/13

The images in this book are used with the permission of: © Shutterstock Images, p. 4; © Ramin Talaie/Corbis, p. 5; © Wikimedia Commons, pp. 6, 13; © Jonathan Feinstein/ Shutterstock Images, p. 7; © AHMAD FAIZAL YAHYA/Shutterstock Images, pp. 9, 14; © Maria J. Avila/MCT/Newscom, p. 11; © Robyn Twomey/Corbis, p.12; © Ian Dagnall/ SuperStock, p. 15; © PRNewsFoto/Newsweek/AP Images, p.17; © Michael Probst/AP Images, p. 18; © Marka/SuperStock, p. 20; © Joi/Wikimedia Commons, p. 21; © Lucky Business/Shutterstock Images, p. 23; © Red Line Editorial, pp. 24, 27; © Pascal Lauener/Reuters/Newscom, p. 26.

Front cover: Courtesy Caterina Fake and Richard Morgenstein/flickr.com (inset); © Kaththea/Dreamstime.com (background).

Main body text set in Adrianna Regular 13/22. Typeface provided by Chank.

CONTENTS

Caterina was born in Pittsburgh, Pennsylvania *(above)*. Her family moved to New Jersey early in her childhood.

HIGHLY GIFTED

Have you ever posted a photograph on the Internet? More than 4.5 million pictures are added to the website Flickr every day. Caterina Fake created Flickr so people could interact. She wanted to create an **online community** where people could share photos and thoughts.

CURIOUS CATERINA

Caterina Fake was born on June 13, 1969. She grew up in
northern New Jersey. Her mother was a pharmacist who had
moved to the United States from the Philippines. Caterina's
father worked in insurance. He taught her about nature and
the stars. Most kids her age grew up watching television. But
Caterina loved spending time reading in the library instead.

Caterina speaks about her websites at a media conference in 2010.

Caterina was smart and curious. She liked to solve puzzles, study butterflies, and read poetry. At the age of eleven, she was accepted into a gifted and talented youth program. Through this weekend program, she took college-level classes in Chinese, biology, and problem solving. She also took painting lessons.

PREPARING FOR COLLEGE

When she was fourteen, Caterina went to Choate Rosemary Hall boarding school in Wallingford, Connecticut. She lived in the dorms at the school. The classes and homework challenged Caterina. It helped her prepare for college.

Caterina took college classes at the Gifted and Talented Program at Montclair State University in New Jersey.

Fake discovered her love of computers while attending Vassar College in New York.

After she graduated in 1986, Fake went to Smith College in Massachusetts. Later, she switched to Vassar College in New York. Here, she studied English literature. Vassar had new technology for the time. The Internet was not yet widely available. But every computer at Vassar was connected to the school intranet. This was the college's network.

Fake could communicate with her classmates from her dorm room computer. Communicating through computers was still a new idea at the time. Caterina was excited. She could send e-mails at any time of day! This was a whole new way to connect with her friends and classmates.

WORLD WIDE WEB

The **World Wide Web (WWW)** was invented in 1989. This new system was a way to connect information online. Linked pages and **search engines** made it easier for everyone to find what they wanted on the Internet. The number of people using the Internet quickly started to grow. In 1991, two years after the WWW was invented, Fake graduated from Vassar.

Fake worked as a painter and a banker after college. But these first jobs weren't the right fit. So in 1994, she decided to move in with her sister in San Francisco, California. All kinds of websites and Internet companies were being created in that part of the country. Fake taught herself how to design websites.

SOCIAL NETWORKING

In 1994, Fake became the art director for Salon.com, a new website. It quickly became a popular current events site.

www.yahoo.com

YAHOO!

 Mail

 News

 Finance

 Sports

 Movies

 omg!

 Shine

 Autos

 Shopping

 Travel

 Dating

Jobs

More Y! Sites ›

All Stories   News   Entertai

Throwback
Floppy Hat
Then. Model A
and Captain H
omg! Celeb New

North Kore
By Ben Bland
take China s
North Korean
Reuters

Submerge
TIBERIAS. Is
archaeolog
ancient life
Associated P

Teacher's Horrific Vid
Cellphone video recorded
exact moment an E-F5 tor
ABC·News (RSS) ↩

Selena
Th

Make YAHOO!
page

Fake helped create an area of the website called Table Talk Forum.

On Table Talk Forum, readers could comment on news articles. People began talking to one another through their comments. This offered a new experience for people at their computers. Fake had helped create one of the first Internet communities with **social networking**. Online discussions were connecting people all over the world!

TECH TALK

"Technology is changing so rapidly. . . . What you thought you were building six months ago is no longer relevant. You have to constantly be alert to what's changing in the world, be able to adapt, and not get too attached to what you're building."

—*Caterina Fake*

With Table Talk Forum, Fake had helped create online communities, which she would continue to develop in the future.

Chapter 2

Caterina Fake and Stewart Butterfield combined their knowledge and interests in technology to create *Game Neverending* and Flickr.

NEW IDEAS

In the late 1990s, the first blogs began getting attention. In these online journals, people could share their interests with the Web. They could type messages or post links to other

websites they liked. Fake created a blog called Caterina.net in 1998. She wrote about art, technology, and her everyday life.

One of her blog followers was Stewart Butterfield. They met at a party in San Francisco in 2000, and the two married the next year. In 2002, they started a company called Ludicorp. Fake and Butterfield wanted to make new technology for the Internet. Their first project was an online game called *Game Neverending*. It focused on interaction between the players.

Stewart Butterfield was also interested in technology and the Internet. He was a computer programmer when he met Fake.

Flickr has more than eight billion photographs!

CREATING FLICKR

In 2004, Fake and Butterfield used some ideas from *Game Neverending* for a new project. The game had let players chat with one another and share pictures. The couple decided to create a website where everyone could interact online. At the time, camera phones were becoming popular. People were sharing pictures with their cell phones.

Fake and Butterfield thought sharing pictures would be a fun way for people to interact on the Internet as well. So they made a website on which people could share pictures. They called it Flickr. Flickr launched in February 2004 at the O'Reilly Emerging Technology Conference. The conference drew attention to the website. Flickr gained nine hundred new members in the first six hours. After that, the number of members grew quickly.

Flickr has come a long way since 2004. Users can view Flickr photos from their cell phones.

FLICKR GROWS

Flickr was not the first photo website. Websites such as Shutterfly already let people store photos online. But Flickr was the first site to make most of the photos public. Anyone could see them. Visitors to the site could search others' photos and leave comments. They could mark their favorite photos. The interaction between users made Flickr an online community. In just six months, Flickr had more than 250,000 users. And more than three million photos were on the website! Companies such as Yahoo! and Google started to take notice.

FLICKR USERS

In the early days of Flickr, all new users were treated as guests at a party. They received e-mails and messages from the company. Flickr wanted people to be involved in the site. Users were taught how to chat online and share photographs. Fake's main goals were bringing people together and getting them to come back. She knew that if they made a personal connection, they would keep coming back.

THE IMMIGRATION WAR • PANDA POLITICS

Newsweek

2006 : $4.50

newsweek.msnbc.com

In April 2006, Fake and Butterfield were on the cover of *Newsweek*, which featured an article about up-and-coming websites.

Putting The 'We' in WEB

NEXT FRONTIERS From MySpace To Flickr and YouTube, User-Generated Sites Are Rocking the Internet

Fake talks to Mark Zuckerberg, founder of Facebook, at the World Economic Forum in Switzerland in 2007.

SELLING TO YAHOO!

Flickr grew so fast that Fake and Butterfield struggled to keep it running smoothly. The site needed upgrades and more workers to help. But those were expensive, and Fake and Butterfield were running out of money. They sold Flickr to the search engine Yahoo! in 2005. It was a solution to their money problems. Yahoo! had many employees to handle the website.

Fake took a job with Yahoo! She led a team that came up with new product ideas. They worked on **social searching**. They were busy coming up with new ideas to improve search engines. Fake learned as much as she could from this group.

TECH TALK

"Our biggest surprise [with Flickr] was what happened when we changed the default photo [option] from a private photo to a public photo. . . . We went from having less than 10 percent of photos public to having more than 80 percent public. By sharing images . . . users are able to see stuff that's going on all over the world."

—Caterina Fake

SOCIAL SEARCHING

Fake was interested in the research Yahoo! was doing on social search. This new kind of search engine used what it knew about someone. It used this information to help find

what the person was searching for. Social search tracked what people searched. Studying the patterns of those searches helped companies such as Yahoo! figure out people's interests.

Then people could type a word into a search engine that used social search and get results that matched those interests. With social search, a search for "food" by someone who often looks for new recipes may turn up a list of cooking websites. Without social search, a search for "food" may just bring up restaurants or pictures of food. What Fake learned about social searching gave her a new idea. On June 13, 2008, Fake left her job at Yahoo! to explore it.

Caterina gave birth to a baby girl in 2007. She used Flickr to share photos of her daughter.

A NEW HUNCH

In 2008, Fake helped start a website called Hunch. The idea behind it was to help people find more of what they like. People would answer questions about themselves. Their answers would help build their profiles. Then Hunch could suggest music, restaurants, games, websites, and more. These suggestions would be based on his or her profile. The website could also offer products to buy. Hunch was meant to be like going to a friend for advice.

At first, it was difficult to get people to answer the profile questions. So Fake made the questions more fun! The

HOW HUNCH WORKS

Behind the scenes, software made use of people's answers. It made connections between people's interests. For example, it might discover that someone liked to watch basketball. The next time this person searched for shoes on Hunch, the site could suggest different pairs of basketball sneakers.

People enjoyed answering Fake's fun questions on Hunch.

website asked people how they cut their sandwiches and if they liked window or aisle seats better on an airplane. Fake designed the questions to make people feel as if they were playing a game.

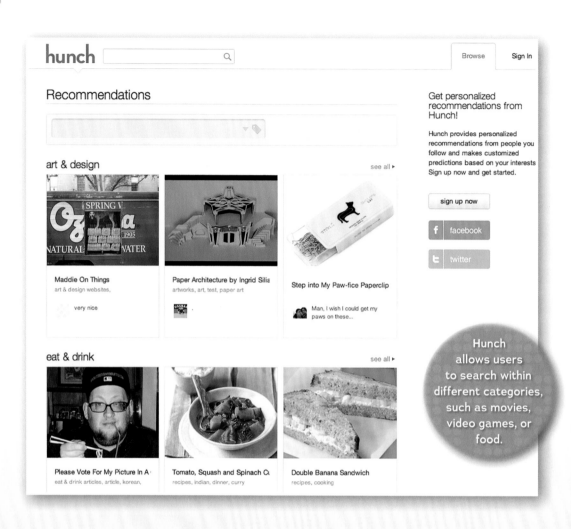

hunch

Browse | Sign In

Recommendations

art & design · see all ▸

Maddie On Things
art & design websites,

very nice

Paper Architecture by Ingrid Silia
artworks, art, test, paper art

Step into My Paw-fice Paperclip

Man, I wish I could get my paws on these...

eat & drink · see all ▸

Please Vote For My Picture In A
eat & drink articles, article, korean,

Tomato, Squash and Spinach Cu
recipes, indian, dinner, curry

Double Banana Sandwich
recipes, cooking

Get personalized recommendations from Hunch!

Hunch provides personalized recommendations from people you follow and makes customized predictions based on your interests Sign up now and get started.

sign up now

f facebook

t twitter

Hunch allows users to search within different categories, such as movies, video games, or food.

The more questions someone answered, the better the profile Hunch created. Most of the users answered more than 150 questions. Fake used the site herself. Hunch suggested restaurants for her to try and movies to see. It even helped her choose which swimsuit to buy!

THE HUNCH PAYS OFF

Fake wanted to help other people start companies. In 2009, she helped create a company called Founder Collective. This company offers advice and funding to new businesses. It helps new companies become successful. Founder Collective helps all kinds of new companies. But Fake especially likes giving advice to new technology companies on the Internet.

Meanwhile, other companies were interested in what she was doing with Hunch. One of those companies was the online auction site eBay. The company wanted to help make shopping easier for its customers, but it needed more information about them. Hunch could help gather that information and make suggestions to customers. On November 21, 2011, eBay bought Hunch for around $80 million.

TECH TALK

"One of the overarching goals of my career has been to make technology more human. . . . You should be able to feel the presence of other people on the Internet."

—Caterina Fake

Fake has always wanted her websites to help bring people together and form online communities.

DIGITAL
MEMORIES

O ne day, Fake was lying under a circle of trees with her daughter. She wanted to mark that spot forever! Some people might do that by carving their initials in a tree or taking a picture. But Fake wanted to create a digital mark.

FINDERY

She made that mark with a new company she created. She called it Findery. In October 2012, she launched the website with twelve employees. On Findery, people can leave digital notes about specific places. Then someone can type in a location to search for it. Findery pulls up a map and any notes people have left about that area. Notes can show events that took place there. People can even leave personal stories about the places they visit.

Findery notes can give a review or share information about a certain place.

Fake combined everything she learned from Flickr, Yahoo!, and Hunch to create Findery. A user can mark another person's note as a favorite. Findery then looks at these notes and favorites to create profiles. For example, a user could mark another user's notes on hot dogs and movies as a favorite. If that person searched "Chicago," restaurants and movie theaters should pop up. Fake works to keep improving how the website makes connections.

Fake's goal is to mix technology with the real world. She designs her websites to be social places where people can leave notes, have conversations, and share ideas. She wants to use the Internet to provide new ways for people to communicate. Fake is always looking for the next way to create a community.

TECH TALK

"[I want to] give the world back to people, have them look up from their devices and see the world around them."

—Caterina Fake

TIMELINE

1969

Caterina Fake is born in Pittsburgh, Pennsylvania, on June 13.

1991

The first web page is created on the World Wide Web. Fake graduates from Vassar College.

1994

Salon.com hires Fake to be its art director.

1998

Fake starts her blog, Caterina.net.

2002

Fake and Stewart Butterfield found Ludicorp.

2004

Fake and Butterfield start Flickr.

2005

Fake begins working for Yahoo! after the company buys Flickr. Fake receives a Best Leaders award from *Business Week* for creating Flickr.

2008

Fake leaves Yahoo! on June 13 to start Hunch.

2009

Fake helps start the company Founder Collective.

2011

eBay buys Hunch on November 21.

2012

Fake launches the website Findery.

GLOSSARY

online community
a group of people who interact online

search engines
computer software that searches data on the Internet

social networking
communicating with others online

social searching
web searching that uses information about someone to find what the person searched for

World Wide Web (WWW)
a system designed with graphics and links to help people find content on the Internet

SOURCE NOTES

10 Teri Evans, "Caterina Fake on Stepping into the Unknown," *Entrepreneur*, March 29, 2011, accessed May 21, 2013, http://www .entrepreneur.com/article/219402.

19 Bronwen Pardes, "Following Intuition: Caterina Fake '91," *Vassar* 105, no. 4 (Fall 2009), accessed July 4, 2013, http://vq.vassar.edu /issues/2009/04/features/following-intuition.html.

25 Devin Leonard, "What You Want: Flickr Creator Spins Addictive New Web Service," *Wired*, July 8, 2010, accessed May 21, 2013, http://www .wired.com/magazine/2010/07/ff_caterina_fake/.

28 Brian Patrick Eha, "Caterina Fake's Findery Aims to Be an 'Adventure Machine,'" *Entrepreneur*, April 3, 2013, accessed June 27, 2013, http:// www.entrepreneur.com/article/226268.

FURTHER INFORMATION

BOOKS

Burns, Jan. *Build Your Online Community: Blogging, Message Boards, Newsgroups, and More*. Berkeley Heights, NJ: Enslow, 2011. Explore many ways to communicate and share ideas online.

Jakubiak, David J. *A Smart Kid's Guide to Social Networking Online*. New York: PowerKids Press, 2010. Read up on smart ways for students to enter the world of social networking.

Kops, Deborah. *Were Early Computers Really the Size of a School Bus?: And Other Questions about Inventions*. Minneapolis: Lerner Publications, 2011. Find out the truth and the myths about clunky early computers and other inventions.

WEBSITES

BrainPOP
http://www.brainpop.com/technology

Play fun games, and learn more about science and engineering!

Flickr
http://www.flickr.com

Look at photographs, and find out more about the company.

Kidblog
http://kidblog.org/home

Create your own blog!

INDEX

ABOUT THE AUTHOR

Patricia Wooster graduated from the University of Kansas with a degree in creative writing. She has written several nonfiction children's books. She lives in Tampa, Florida, with her husband, Scot, and two boys, Max and Jack.